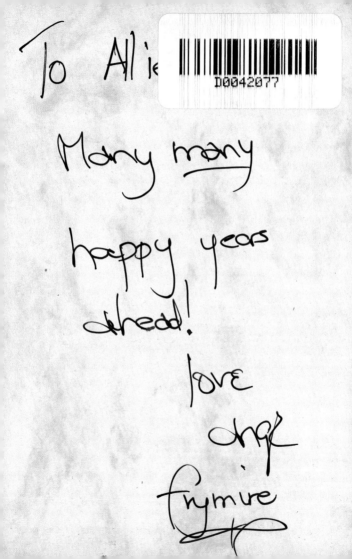

To Allie

Many many

happy years

ahead!

love

Angie

Frymire

Other Giftbooks by Exley
Happiness Quotations   **Wishing you Happiness**
Garden Lover's Quotations   **Flowers a Celebration**

Published simultaneously in 1995 by Exley Publications in Great
Britain, and Exley Giftbooks in the USA.

For Richard.

24 23 22 21 20 19 18 17 16 15 14

ISBN 1-85015-647-6

Edited and pictures selected by Helen Exley.

Picture research by Image Select International.
Typeset by Delta, Watford.
Printed in China.

Exley Publications Ltd., 16 Chalk Hill, Watford, Herts WD19 4BG.
Exley Publications LLC, 185 Main Street, Spencer, MA 01562, USA.
www.helenexleygiftbooks.com

Acknowledgements: The publishers are grateful for permission to reproduce copyright
material. While every effort has been made to trace copyright holders, the publishers would
be pleased to hear from any not here acknowledged. WENDELL BERRY: from "Openings"
© 1968 by Wendell Berry, published by Harcourt Brace Jovanovich Inc.; RACHEL
CARSON: from "The Sense of Wonder" copyright © 1956 by Rachel L. Carson. Copyright ©
renewed 1984 by Roger Christie. Reprinted by permission of Frances Collin Literary
Agency; THICH NHAT HANH: extracts from "Being Peace", published by Parallax Press,
1987; PHILIP KAPLEAU: from "The Wheel Of Life And Death; published by Doubleday, a
division of Bantam Doubleday Dell Publishing Group Inc., 1989; ALICE KOLLER: Extract
from "The Stations of Solitude", published by Bantam Doubleday Dell. © Alice Koller 1990.
Reprinted by permission of Alice Koller. JAMES A. MICHENER: from "The Fires of Spring"
published by Martin Secker and Warberg Ltd.; W. B. YEATS: "The Lake Isle of Innisfree"
from "The Poems of W. B. Yeats: A New Edition" edited by Richard J. Finneran. Reprinted
by permission of A. P. Watt Ltd. on behalf of Michael Yeats.
Picture credits: Archiv für Kunst (AKG), Bridgeman Art Library (BAL), Christie's Colour
Library (CCL), Edimedia (EDM), Scala (SCA), Statens Konstmuseer (SK). Cover: © 1995
Alexandr Michajlowitsch Gerassimow, Russian State Museum, St. Petersburg, AKG; title
page: © 1995 John Gwendolen, Paris, Sheffield City Art Galleries, BAL; page 6: AKG; page
9: AKG; page 10: © 1995 Hans Andersen Brendekilde, Bonhams London, BAL; page 12:
AKG; page 15: SCA; page 16: © 1995 Solsken V. Johansen, SK; page 18: © 1995 Justus
Lundegard, SK; page 21: © 1995 James Herbert Snell, Bourne Gallery, FAP; page 22: as
cover; page 24: © 1995 Julian Novorol, Private collection, BAL; page 26: BAL; page 28: BAL;
page 30: © 1995 Laurito Andersen Ring, Oslo National Gallery, BAL; page 32: © 1995 Joyce
Haddon, Private collection, BAL; page 34: © 1995 Henry Hubert La Thangue, Bradford Art
Galleries and Museums, BAL; page 36: © 1995 Carl Larsson, SK; page 38: SCA; page 40:
BAL; page 42: SCA; page 45: © 1995 Franziska Geiger-Weishaupt, Laubgang, State Gallery,
Karlsruhe, AKG; page 47: © 1995 Paul Hey, AKG; page 49: CCL; page 50: BAL; page 52:
EDM; page 54: AKG; page 57: SCA, page 58: SCA; page 60: © 1995 Charles Oppenheimer,
Oldam Art Gallery, BAL.

Thoughts on...
BEING
AT PEACE

WORDS AND PAINTINGS
SELECTED BY
HELEN EXLEY

⧉EXLEY

All real and wholesome enjoyments possible to man have been just as possible to him, since first he was made of the earth, as they are now: and they are possible to him chiefly in peace. To watch the corn grow, and

the blossoms set; to draw hard breath over
ploughshare or spade; to read, to think, to love,
to hope, to pray – these are the things that
make men happy.

JOHN RUSKIN (1819-1900)

If you want to be happy, be.

LEO TOLSTOY (1828-1910)

You do not need to leave your room … Remain sitting at your table and listen. Do not even listen, simply wait. Do not even wait, be quite still and solitary. The world will freely offer itself to you to be unmasked. It has no choice. It will roll in ecstasy at your feet.

FRANZ KAFKA

We need time to dream, time to remember, and time to reach the infinite. Time to be.

GLADYS TABER

I used to believe that anything was better than nothing. Now I know that sometimes nothing is better.

GLENDA JACKSON, b.1936

All our miseries derive from not being able to sit quietly in a room alone.

BLAISE PASCAL (1623-1662)

He [the American Indian] believes profoundly in silence – the sign of a perfect equilibrium. Silence is the absolute poise or balance of body, mind and spirit. The man who preserves his selfhood ever calm and unshaken by the storms of existence – not a leaf as it were, astir on the trees; not a ripple upon the surface of a shining pool – his, in the mind of the unlettered sage, is the ideal attitude and conduct of life.

OHIYESA [CHARLES ALEXANDER EASTMAN]

There is a silence
into which the world cannot intrude.
There is an ancient peace
you carry in your heart
and have not lost.

A COURSE IN MIRACLES

Those who contemplate the beauty of the earth
find reserves of strength that will endure as
long as life lasts.
There is symbolic as well as actual beauty
in the migration of the birds, the ebb
and flow of the tides, the folded bud

ready for the spring.
There is something infinitely healing in
the repeated refrains of nature – the assurance
that dawn comes after night, and spring after
the winter.

RACHEL CARSON (1907-1964)

These roses under my window make no
reference to former roses or to better ones;
they are for what they are; they exist with
God today. There is no time to them.
There is simply the rose; it is perfect in
every moment of its existence.
Before a leaf-bud has burst, its whole life acts;
in the full-blown flower there is no more;
in the leafless root there is no less.
Its nature is satisfied, and it satisfies nature, in
all moments alike. There is no time to it.
But man postpones or remembers; he does
not live in the present, but with reverted eye
laments the past, or, heedless of the riches
that surround him, stands on tiptoe
to foresee the future. He cannot be happy
and strong until he too lives with nature in the
present, above time.

RALPH WALDO EMERSON (1803-1882),
FROM "SELF-RELIANCE"

We are so busy we hardly have time to look at the people we love, even in our own household, and to look at ourselves. Society is organized in a way that even when we have some leisure time, we don't know how to use it to get back in touch with ourselves. We have millions of ways to lose this precious time – we turn on the TV or pick up the telephone, or start the car and go somewhere.

We are not used to being with ourselves, and we act as if we don't like ourselves and are trying to escape from ourselves.

THICH NHAT HANH,
FROM *"SUFFERING IS NOT ENOUGH"*

We collect data, things, people, ideas, "profound experiences", never penetrating any of them … But there are other times. There are times when we stop. We sit still. We lose ourselves in a pile of leaves or its memory. We listen and breezes from a whole other world begin to whisper.

JAMES CARROLL, b.1943

A single gentle rain makes the grass many shades greener. So our prospects brighten on the influx of better thoughts. We should be blessed if we lived in the present always, and took advantage of every accident that befell us, like the grass which confesses the influence of

the slightest dew that falls on it; and did not spend our time in atoning for the neglect of past opportunities, which we call doing our duty. We loiter in winter while it is already spring.

HENRY DAVID THOREAU (1817-1862)

I will arise and go now, and go to Innisfree,
And a small cabin build there, of clay
  and wattles made:
Nine bean-rows will I have there, a hive
  for the honeybee,
And live alone in the bee-loud glade.

And I shall have some peace there,
  for peace comes dropping slow,
Dropping from the veils of the morning
  to where the cricket sings;
There midnight's all a glimmer, and
  noon a purple glow,
And evening full of the linnet's wings.

I will arise and go now, for always
  night and day
I hear lake water lapping with low sounds
  by the shore;
While I stand on the roadway, or on
  the pavements grey,
I hear it in the deep heart's core.

WILLIAM BUTLER YEATS (1865-1939),
FROM *"THE LAKE ISLE OF INNISFREE"*

We tend to be alive in the future, not now. We say, "Wait until I finish school and get my Ph.D degree, and then I will be really alive." When we have it, and it's not easy to get, we say to ourselves, "I have to wait until I have a job in order to be *really* alive." And then after the job, a car. After the car, a house. We are not capable of being alive in the present moment. We tend to postpone being alive to the future, the distant future, we don't know when. Now is not the moment to be alive. We may never be alive at all in our entire life.

THICH NHAT HANH,
FROM "*SUFFERING IS NOT ENOUGH*"

It's easy enough to say that life is a process. Yet how many of us live our life as if it is a product? When we get or have what we want: a better job, a new place to live, thinner, smarter, older (younger?), serenity, peace, etc., etc., then we'll really have something. Then our lives will be worth living. The only known destination in life is death, and even dying is a process.

JAN JOHNSON DRANTELL

Peace is when time doesn't matter
as it passes by.

MARIA SCHELL, QUOTED IN "TIME", MARCH 3, 1958

What a fine lesson is conveyed to the mind – to
take no note of time but by its benefits, to

watch only for the smiles and neglect the frowns of fate, to compose our lives of bright and gentle moments, turning always to the sunny side of things, and letting the rest slip from our imaginations, unheeded or forgotten.

WILLIAM HAZLITT (1778-1830)

To fill the hour – that is happiness; to fill the hour, and leave no crevice for a repentance or an approval.

RALPH WALDO EMERSON (1803-1882)

Living the past is a dull and lonely business, looking back strains the neck muscles, causes you to bump into people not going your way.

EDNA FERBER (1887-1968)

I do not believe in recovery. The past, with its pleasures, its rewards, its foolishness, its punishments, is there for each of us for ever, and it should be.

LILLIAN HELLMAN (1907-1984)

The dream was always running ahead of one. To catch up, to live for a moment in unison with it, that was the miracle.

ANAÏS NIN (1903-1977)

Nor land nor yet living belongs unto me,
Yet I can go out in the meadows and see
The healthy green grass – and behold
the shower fall,
As the wealth of that being that blesses us all.
And he that feels this, who can say he is poor?
For fortune's the birthright of joy
– nothing more.
And he that feels thus takes the wealth
from the soil,
For the miser owns nought but the trouble
and toil.

JOHN CLARE (1793-1864)

Why should we be in such desperate haste
to succeed, and in such desperate enterprises?
If a man cannot keep pace with his
companions, perhaps it is because he hears
a different drummer.
Let him step to the music which he hears,
however measured or far away. We will not be
shipwrecked on a vain reality.

HENRY DAVID THOREAU (1817-1862)

Like water which can clearly mirror the
sky and the trees only so long as its surface
is undisturbed, the mind can only reflect
the true image of the Self when it is tranquil
and wholly relaxed.

INDRA DEVI

I would like to live ... open to time and death painlessly, noticing everything, remembering nothing, choosing the given with a fierce and pointed will.

ANNIE DILLARD

The lure of the distant and the difficult is deceptive. The great opportunity is where you are.

JOHN BURROUGHS (1837-1921)

For the past eighty years I have started
each day in the same manner. It is not a
mechanical routine but something essential to
my daily life. I go to the piano, and I play
two preludes and fugues of Bach.
I cannot think of doing otherwise. It is
a sort of benediction on the house. But
that is not its only meaning for me. It is
a rediscovery of the world of which I have
the joy of being a part. It fills me with
awareness of the wonder of life, with a
feeling of the incredible marvel of being
a human being.

PABLO CASALS (1876-1973),
FROM *"JOYS AND SORROWS"*

A man's best things are nearest him,
lie close about his feet.

RICHARD MONCKTON MILNES (1809-1885)

Nothing is worth more than this day.

JOHANN WOLFGANG VON GOETHE (1749-1832)

To be reborn hourly and daily in this life, we need to die – to give of ourselves wholly to the demands of the moment, so that we utterly "disappear". Thoughts of past, present, or future, of life and death, of this world and the next, are transcended in the superabundance of the now. Time and timelessness coalesce: this is the moment of eternity. Thus our every act is a matter either of giving life or taking it away. If we perform each act with total absorption, we give life to our life. If we do things half-heartedly, we kill that life.

PHILIP KAPLEAU

Yesterday is a cancelled cheque; tomorrow is a promissory note; today is the only cash you have – so spend it wisely.

KAY LYONS

Let us spend one day as deliberately as nature, and not be thrown off the track by every nutshell and mosquito's wing that falls on the rails. Let us rise early and fast, or break fast, gently and without perturbation; let company come and let company go, let the bells ring and

the children cry – determined to make a day
of it. If the engine whistles, let it whistle till
it is hoarse for its pains.
If the bell rings, why should we run?
Time is but the stream I go a-fishing in.

HENRY DAVID THOREAU (1817-1862)

To every thing there is a season, and a time
to every purpose under the heaven: a time
to be born, and a time to die; a time to plant,
and a time to pluck up that which is planted;
a time to kill, and a time to heal; a time to
break down, and a time to build up; a time
to weep, and a time to laugh; a time to mourn,
and a time to dance; a time to cast away
stones, and a time to gather stones together;
a time to embrace, and a time to refrain from
embracing; a time to get, and a time to lose;
a time to keep, and a time to cast away; a
time to rend, and a time to sew; a time to
keep silence, and a time to speak; a time to
love, and a time to hate; a time of war, and
a time of peace.

ECCLESIASTES 3, 1-8

If only I may grow: firmer, simpler
– quieter, warmer.

DAG HAMMARSKJÖLD

Let us not therefore go hurrying about and
collecting honey, bee-like, buzzing here and
there impatiently from a knowledge of what is
to be arrived at. But let us open out leaves like
a flower, and be passive and receptive:
budding patiently under the eye of Apollo and
taking hints from every noble insect that
favours us with a visit.

JOHN KEATS (1795-1821)

Books are the quietest and most constant
of friends; they are the most accessible
and wisest of counselors, and the most
patient of teachers.

CHARLES W. ELIOT (1834-1926)

THE PEACE OF WILD THINGS

When despair for the world grows in me and I wake in the night at the least sound in fear of what my life and my children's lives may be, I go and lie down where the wood drake rests in his beauty on the water, and the great heron feeds.

I come into the peace of wild things who
do not tax their lives with forethought of grief.
I come into the presence of still water. And
I feel above me day-blind stars waiting for their
light. For a time I rest in the grace
of the world, and am free.

WENDELL BERRY, b.1934

I leave this notice on my door
For each accustomed visitor:
"I am gone into the fields
To take what this sweet hour yields;
Reflection, you may come tomorrow,
Sit by the fireside of Sorrow.
You with the unpaid bill, Despair,
You tiresome verse-reciter, Care,
I will pay you in the grave,
Death will listen, to your stave.
Expectation, too, be off!
Today is for itself enough."

PERCY BYSSHE SHELLEY (1792-1822)

Work is not always required of a man. There is
such a thing as sacred idleness, the cultivation
of which is now fearfully neglected.

GEORGE MACDONALD

Over all the mountaintops
Is peace.
In all treetops
You perceive scarcely a breath.
The little birds in the forest
Are silent.
Wait then; soon
You, too, will have peace.

**JOHANN WOLFGANG VON GOETHE,
FROM "WANDERERS NACHTLIED"**

To a mind that is still the whole
universe surrenders.

CHUANG TZU

Sitting quietly, doing nothing,
Spring comes, and the grass
grows by itself.

ZENRIN POEM

The poor long for riches and the
rich for heaven, but the wise long
for a state of tranquillity.

SWAMI RAMA

"If it were just a matter of playing football with the firmament, stirring up the ocean, turning back rivers, carrying away mountains, seizing the moon, moving the Pole-star or shifting a planet, I could manage it easily enough.

Even if it were a question of my head being cut off and the brain removed or my belly being ripped open and my heart cut out … I would take on the job at once," said Monkey. "But if it comes to sitting still and meditating, I am bound to come off badly. It's quite against my nature to sit still."

WU CH'ÊNG-EN

To preserve the silence within – amid all the noise. To remain open and quiet … no matter how many tramp across the parade-ground in whirling dust under an arid sky.

DAG HAMMARSKJÖLD

Change is an easy panacea. It takes character to stay in one place and be happy there.

ELIZABETH CLARKE DUNN

Let your mind be quiet, realizing the beauty of the world, and the immense, the boundless treasures that it holds in store. All that you have within you, all that your heart desires, all that your nature so specially fits you for – that or the counterpart of it waits embedded in the great whole, for you. It will

surely come to you. Yet equally surely not one moment before its appointed time will it come. All your crying and fever and reaching out of hands will make no difference.

Therefore do not begin that game at all.

EDWARD CARPENTER

And David thought:"It's like coming home to yourself at last."

For this is the journey that men make: to find themselves. If they fail in this, it doesn't matter much what else they find. Money, position, fame, many loves, revenge, are all of little consequence, and when the tickets are collected at the end of the ride, they are tossed into the bin marked FAILURE.

But if a man happens to find himself – if he knows what he can be depended upon to do, the limits of his courage, the positions from which he will no longer retreat, the degree to which he can surrender his inner life to some woman, the secret reservoirs of his determination, the extent of his dedication, the depth of his feeling for beauty, his honest and unpostured goals – then he has found a mansion which he can inhabit with dignity all the days of his life.

JAMES A. MICHENER (1907-1997), FROM *"THE FIRES OF SPRING"*

When King Pyrrus prepared for his expedition into Italy, his wise counsellor Cyneas, to make him sensible of the vanity of his ambition: "Well, sir," said he, " to what end do you make all this mighty preparation?" "To make myself master of Italy," replied the King. "And what after that is done?" said Cyneas. "I will pass over into Gaul and Spain," said the other. "And what then?" "I will then go to subdue Africa; and lastly, when I have brought the whole world to my subjection, I will sit down and rest content at my own ease." "For God sake, sir," replied Cyneas, "tell me what hinders that you may not, if you please, be now in the condition you speak of? Why do you not now at this instant, settle yourself in the state you seem to aim at, and spare all the labour and hazard you interpose?"

MICHEL DE MONTAIGNE (1533-1592), FROM *"ESSAYS"*

If we are not happy, if we are not peaceful, we cannot share peace and happiness with others, even those we love, those who live under the same roof. If we are peaceful, if we are happy, we can smile and blossom like a flower, and everyone in our family, our entire society, will benefit from our peace.

THICH NHAT HANH, FROM *"BEING PEACE"*

I know not how it is with you
I love the first and last,
The whole field of the present view,
The whole flow of the past.

One tittle of the things that are,
Nor you should change nor I -
One pebble in our path – one star
In all our heaven of sky.

ROBERT LOUIS STEVENSON (1850-1894)

If it be my lot to crawl, I will crawl contentedly: if to fly, I will fly with alacrity; but as long as I can possibly avoid it, I will never be unhappy.

SYDNEY SMITH (1771-1845)

I surround myself with silence. The silence is within me, permeates my house, reaches beyond the surfaces of the outer walls and into the bordering woods. It is one silence, continuous from within me outward in all directions:... In the silence I listen, I watch, I sense, I attend, I

observe. I require this silence. I search it out.

ALICE KOLLER

And silence, like a poultice, comes
To heal the blows of sound.

OLIVER WENDELL HOLMES (1809-1884)

In the midst of winter, I finally learned that there was in me an invincible summer.

ALBERT CAMUS (1913-1960)

Until you make peace with who you are, you'll never be content with what you have.

DORIS MORTMAN

Contentment comes as the infallible result of great acceptances, great humilities – of not trying to make ourselves this or that, but of surrendering ourselves to the fullness of life – of letting life flow through us.

DAVID GRAYSON (1870-1946)

Joy exists only in self acceptance. Seek perfect acceptance, not a perfect life.

AUTHOR UNKNOWN

I have enough for this life. If there is no other life, then this one has been enough to make it worth being born, myself a human being.

PEARL S. BUCK (1892-1973)